MEET
BENJAMIN FRANKLIN

MEET
BENJAMIN FRANKLIN

★ ★ ★ ★

By Maggi Scarf
Illustrated by Pat Fogarty

STEP-UP BOOKS

Random House 🏠 New York

To Martha, Betsy, and Susie

Illustration on page 6 courtesy of the New York Public Library Picture Collection.

First paperback edition, 1989

Library of Congress Cataloging-in-Publication Data:
Scarf, Maggi. Meet Benjamin Franklin / written by Maggi Scarf ; illustrated by Pat Fogarty. p. cm.—(Step-up biographies) SUMMARY: A biography of Benjamin Franklin highlighting his inventions, his newspaper and almanac, his work on the Declaration of Independence, and his diplomatic trips to England and France on behalf of the colonies. ISBN: 0-394-81961-6 (pbk.); 0-394-91961-0 (lib. bdg.)
1. Franklin, Benjamin, 1706–1790—Juvenile literature. 2. Statesmen—United States—Biography—Juvenile literature. [1. Franklin, Benjamin, 1706–1790. 2. Statesmen.
3. Inventors.] I. Fogarty, Pat, ill. II. Title. III. Series. E302.6.F8S35 1989
973.3'092'4—dc19 [B] 88-17657

Manufactured in the United States of America

0

CONTENTS

1
MEET BENJAMIN FRANKLIN

Benjamin Franklin was one of the most important men of his time. He was a poor boy. He went to school for only two years. But he became America's first famous scientist, inventor, and writer. And he was one of the great leaders of the American Revolution.

Franklin made new friends for his country everywhere he went. He became known and loved all over the world.

Benjamin Franklin's father was born in

England. About the year 1683 he left home and crossed the sea to English lands in America.

These lands were along the coast of the Atlantic Ocean. They were called colonies. They were ruled by the English king.

The colonies did not have much to do with each other. Each one had its own government. Towns were small and far apart. Sometimes it took less time to send a letter all the way to England than to another colony.

Beyond the colonies America was a huge and unknown country. Few people but Indians lived there.

Benjamin's father went to live in the town of Boston, in the colony of Massachusetts. There he made soap and candles. And he had a very big family. Benjamin was the fifteenth of his 17 children.

Ben was born on January 17, 1706. He was born in a little house on Milk Street in Boston.

He was a happy child. There were always things to do with his many brothers and sisters. He was bright, too. He loved to read. But he did not have many books. And he could not go to school for long. He had to help his father in the candle shop.

But Ben did not work all the time. He had lots of time to play, too.

2

THE YOUNG PRINTER

One day Ben was flying his kite next to a pond. He decided to go for a swim. He tied the kite string to a stick in the ground.

While Ben was in the water, he watched the kite pull at the string. Then he had an idea. He untied the string. He held on to it and got back into the water. The kite towed him quickly for almost a mile across the pond.

When Ben was about 12, his father decided he should learn some kind of work. Ben wanted to be a sailor. But that was one thing his father would not let him do. Ben's older brother Josiah had gone to sea. He had been drowned.

Ben and his father went on long walks together. They watched people doing many different kinds of work. Because Ben liked books so much, they decided he should be a printer.

Another of Ben's older brothers, James, was a printer. Ben went to work for him.

At first he was very happy. He liked his new job. There were many newspapers and books in the shop. He used every spare minute to read. He read early in the morning before work. He read late at night after work. He read at lunchtime and on Sundays. He taught himself to be a fine writer. He learned arithmetic. Ben had a quick and lively mind.

When Ben was 15, James started a newspaper. It was called *The New England Courant.*

Many of James's friends wrote for the newspaper. Ben wanted to write something too. He knew his big brother would not print anything written by such a young boy. But he decided to try.

3

THE RUNAWAY

Ben wrote a letter to *The New England Courant.* Secretly, he slipped it under the printing shop door at night. He did not sign it with his own name. He signed it "Silence Dogood."

James and his friends thought it was very funny. James printed it in his newspaper. Ben smiled when they wondered who Silence Dogood could be.

Ben kept his secret well. He wrote many

more letters to the newspaper. He signed them all Silence Dogood.

Silence Dogood was supposed to be an old woman who lived out in the country. She had bright and funny things to say about everything. No one dreamed that she was really young Benjamin Franklin.

Ben liked to listen to James and his friends laughing at the Silence Dogood letters. At last he told them he had written them. They were all amazed!

But James was not happy about it. He thought Ben was showing off. The brothers began to argue all the time. James even began to beat Ben.

Ben knew he could not go on working for his brother. He asked James to let him work for someone else. But James said no.

Ben decided to run away.

He found a ship that was going to New York. The captain agreed to take him along. Ben sold his books to raise a little

money. And in the fall of 1723 he sailed away.

It took three days to get to New York. As soon as he got there, he looked for work as a printer. But he could not find a job anywhere. A man told him to go to Philadelphia, in the colony of Pennsylvania. He said Ben could find work there.

4

ON TO PHILADELPHIA

Ben had to take another boat from New York. It had not gone far when a storm came up. The wind tore the sails to pieces. The waves tossed the boat about. Suddenly a man fell into the sea. Quickly Ben reached down into the water. He grabbed the man by his hair and pulled him back into the boat.

The wind began to blow the boat out to sea. The people in it had to drop the anchor. They stayed in one place for 30 hours. They were cold and wet. They had nothing to eat. And all they had to drink was a bottle of old, dirty rum.

Finally the wind died down. The boat landed in New Jersey. Ben was glad to get off. But he still had a long way to go.

Ben spent the next day walking through the rain. He walked for 50 miles. He walked all the way across New Jersey.

It was a long, hard trip. Ben began to

wish he had never run away from his brother James.

At last Ben came to a town by the Delaware River. There he hoped to find a boat going to Philadelphia.

But Ben found that there was no boat leaving for three days.

That evening he took a walk by the river. A small boat came by. The people in it said they would take him to Philadelphia.

There was no wind. They had to row. Ben helped. They rowed until midnight. Then they stopped and camped on shore for the night.

Early the next day Ben Franklin reached Philadelphia. It was a cold Sunday morning in October. Ben was tired. And he felt very much alone in the strange city.

5

BEN SETS UP SHOP

Ben walked around the streets for a while. He was very hungry. A boy showed him the way to a bakery.

Ben asked the baker to sell him some bread. The baker handed him three big rolls. Ben's pockets were full of his socks and shirts. He had nowhere to put the rolls.

Ben put one roll under one arm and one roll under the other arm. Then he walked along the street, eating the third roll.

A young woman named Deborah Read was standing in a doorway. She saw Ben walking down the street. He looked very funny with his bulging pockets and his fat rolls. Deborah giggled. She stared after him until he was gone from sight.

Ben went to work with a printer named Mr. Keimer. He found Ben a place to live. It was in the house of Deborah Read's father. Deborah and Ben soon grew to like each other very much.

Ben was very happy. He had many new friends. The one man who did not like him was Mr. Keimer. But Ben was the best worker that Mr. Keimer had. Soon Mr. Keimer put him in charge of the whole shop.

Mr. Keimer was an odd man. He had many strange ideas. Ben often teased him about them. Mr. Keimer did not like this at all.

As time went on, things got worse and worse between them.

One day there was a lot of noise out in the street. Ben leaned out the window to see what it was. Mr. Keimer saw him. He yelled at Ben to get back to work. Ben was very angry. He yelled right back. Mr. Keimer told him he was fired. Ben picked up his hat and walked out.

That night there was a knock on Ben's door. It was a friend of his from Mr. Keimer's shop. He wanted to start a new printing shop with Ben. Ben agreed to try.

Early in 1728 their shop opened. At first they did not have much to do. But Ben was the best printer in Pennsylvania. Soon he was busy all the time.

6

HEALTHY, WEALTHY, AND WISE

On September 1, 1730, Benjamin Franklin married Deborah Read. He took her to live in the house where he had his printing shop.

Ben was busier than ever. He had started his own newspaper. It was called *The Pennsylvania Gazette.* He wrote most of it himself.

Everyone liked *The Pennsylvania Gazette.* Ben wrote well. And what he wrote was often very funny.

At the same time, Franklin was given a very important job. He was made printer for the Pennsylvania Assembly.

The men in the Assembly were chosen by the people. Assemblymen made the colony's laws. They also made a lot of speeches. Copies of the laws and the speeches had to be printed. This was Franklin's job.

In 1732 Franklin started a new almanac. This almanac was a book about all kinds of things. It told about the stars. It told about the moon and tides. It had a calendar. It told people how to cook. It was full of jokes and stories. It even told what the weather would be for the year to come.

Franklin called it *Poor Richard's Almanack*. He pretended a poor farmer named Richard Saunders had written it. Before long people all through the colonies knew Poor Richard's sayings. They laughed at the funny ones like, "Three can keep a secret if two are dead." They liked the wise ones like, "Early to bed and early to rise, makes a man healthy, wealthy, and wise."

Poor Richard became famous in other countries too. In France he was called "Bonhomme Richard."

Franklin was always thinking of new ways to do things. He liked to show people how to work together.

There were no fire fighters in the city of Philadelphia. Sometimes there were terrible fires. Many houses burned to the ground.

Franklin thought that something should be done. He said that the city should have a fire company. He wrote about it in his newspaper.

Right away, everyone wanted to be a fire fighter. There were too many men for one fire company. So more were started. Soon Philadelphia was one of the safest cities in the world.

7

FRANKLIN'S FAMOUS FIREPLACE

Ben and Deborah were very happy
together. They had two fine sons. The
older boy was named William. The
younger was named Francis. In 1736
Francis was four years old.

Often a terrible sickness spread through
the colonies. It was called smallpox. Many
people died. Little Francis caught smallpox. Ben and Deborah sat with him day
and night. They did everything they could
for him. But nothing helped.

After a few days Francis died.

The death of his little boy was a great blow to Franklin. It took him a long time to get over it. But he never stopped thinking of ways to make life better for other people.

In those days most houses were very cold in the winter. The only warm place in a room was right by a fireplace. This was because most of the hot air from the fire went up the chimney.

Fireplaces often made the whole room smoky. And they used up a lot of wood. They were dangerous, too. People had to stay close to them to keep warm. Sometimes sparks would set fire to their clothes.

Franklin invented a new and much better fireplace. He called it the Pennsylvania Fireplace. But most people called it the Franklin stove.

All the smoke from the Franklin stove went up the chimney. All the hot air went out into the room. It used less wood. And it had a door to keep sparks from flying out.

Soon people all over the colonies were using Franklin stoves.

8

FRANKLIN GIVES
HIS FRIENDS A SHOCK

In 1746 Franklin saw something new and wonderful. It was called a Leyden jar. It was a jar half-filled with water. The inside and outside of the jar were lined with metal foil. A wire ran into the jar. Anyone who touched the wire saw a flash and got an electric shock.

Franklin was very excited. He told his friends about it. Soon everyone wanted to feel an electric shock.

No one knew what electricity was.

Franklin went to work to find out more about it.

Franklin worked day and night. He used things from around the house. He made the first electric battery with some pieces of window glass and metal. He made little machines that set off electric

sparks. He read all he could about electricity. Soon Franklin knew more about it than anyone in America.

Most people thought of electricity as just a toy. But Franklin thought of ways to put it to use.

Franklin told his friends about his plans for an "electric picnic." They would kill a turkey with an electric shock. Then they would cook the turkey over a fire started by an electric spark.

After the picnic they would use the electric battery to fire off guns. And they would all drink to this strange new thing called electricity.

Franklin went on working with electricity. He saw that it was very much like lightning. Both of them moved in the same way. Both gave out a bright light. And both could start fires.

Franklin wondered if they could be the same thing. He decided to find out.

9
FRANKLIN TAMES LIGHTNING

Franklin knew that electricity was drawn to a metal point. He knew that it would travel along a piece of cotton. And he knew that it was stopped by silk. Now he wondered if lightning would act the same way.

One day in June of 1752 Franklin and his son, William, went out in a storm. Franklin had a kite. There was a metal point on it. Franklin flew the kite high up into the sky.

The kite had a cotton string. On the end of the string, he tied a key and a piece of silk. He held on to the silk and waited.

At first nothing happened.

Suddenly tiny threads of cotton began to stick out along the string. But Franklin did not feel anything. He touched the key. He felt a shock!

Lightning had gone to the metal point. It had gone down the cotton string. It had been stopped by the piece of silk. It had done just what electricity does. Franklin had proved that they are the same thing.

It was an amazing discovery. But it was dangerous, too. Even Franklin did not know how dangerous it was. He was lucky a big bolt of lightning had not hit his kite. It would have killed him.

People all over the world heard about Franklin's great discovery. Benjamin Franklin was famous.

Right away Franklin thought of a way to use his discovery.

Lightning often hit houses and set them on fire. Franklin thought of putting pointed metal rods on the tops of houses. The rods would draw off the lightning in the air. Then houses would not be hit. Franklin wrote about this in his newspaper and in *Poor Richard's Almanack.*

Soon the new lightning rods were put up on houses everywhere. And they worked. Fewer houses were hit by lightning. Many lives were saved. Franklin

had made another great discovery. People called him the man who tamed lightning.

Franklin was now 46 years old. He was known and loved all over the city of Philadelphia. He had done many things for the city. He had started a college. He had started the city's first hospital. He was now an assemblyman, too. And he was in charge of the mail in Philadelphia.

In 1753 Franklin became deputy postmaster general of America. He was in charge of all the mail in the northern colonies.

At that time post offices were not run well at all. The mail did not go out very often. Letters were carried by men on horseback. It took a long time for them to get from one place to another.

Franklin rode all over the colonies looking at the post offices. He hired many more mail riders. He showed them the best roads to take. He sent the mail out more often. Mail service became much faster and better.

More and more people began to use the mail. Letters and newspapers went from one colony to another. The people began to feel closer to each other. The colonies did not seem so far apart anymore.

10

TROUBLES OVER TAXES

Franklin was working hard as an assemblyman, too. There were many quarrels in the Assembly. Most of them were about money and taxes.

Most of Pennsylvania belonged to a family named Penn. The Penns lived in England. They did not pay taxes on their land in America.

Franklin thought that the Penns should pay taxes like everyone else. So did many other assemblymen.

In 1757 the assemblymen asked Franklin to go to England. They hoped he could get the Penns to pay the taxes.

Franklin agreed to go. He and Deborah had a little girl now. Her name was Sally. She stayed home with her mother. Franklin took his son, William, with him to London.

There Franklin went to talk to the Penns. But they would not listen. They did not want to pay any taxes.

Franklin knew it would be a long fight. He wrote about the taxes in English newspapers. He went to see all the important people he could. He told them that everyone who had land in America should pay taxes.

Franklin was a good talker. And he was a great writer. People began to think he was right. After two long years the Penns agreed to pay their taxes.

Franklin loved England. He stayed on

for three more years. He and William traveled all over. He met many famous men. He made many new friends.

In 1762 Franklin went home to Philadelphia. He was 57 years old. He had worked hard. He hoped he could rest awhile.

But Franklin was not at home for long. There was more trouble with the Penns. Again the assemblymen asked him to go to England.

Franklin asked Deborah and Sally to come with him. But Deborah did not want to leave home. William was now governor of New Jersey. This time Franklin would have to go to England alone.

Franklin and Deborah said good-bye sadly. They did not know how long he would be away. They did not know if they would ever see each other again.

In England, Franklin found worse trouble than the trouble with the Penns.

There was a new law that made the colonies pay more taxes. It was called the Stamp Act.

The Stamp Act put a tax on all kinds of papers. It taxed almanacs. It taxed newspapers. It even taxed playing cards.

Most Americans did not want to pay the new taxes. They wrote angry letters to the English government.

Franklin agreed with the letters. He felt Americans should be free to make their own taxes. He worked hard against the Stamp Act.

The English decided they would have to listen to the Americans. They called a meeting. And they asked Benjamin Franklin to tell the American side of the story.

Franklin told the English that the Americans would never pay the new tax. He told them that the Americans would fight before they would pay it.

The English believed him. A few days later the government stopped the hated Stamp Act.

When the news got to America, there was great excitement. People cheered. Church bells rang out. Everyone knew what Franklin had done. He was a hero.

11

FRANKLIN STANDS ALONE

Franklin became very famous in England. People began to think of him as a kind of magician. They thought he could do anything.

One day Franklin was out walking with some friends. They came to a pond. Franklin decided to play a joke on them. He held his cane up over the waves. He said some magic words. The water became still.

Franklin's friends did not know what to think. Franklin laughed. He showed them how he had done it.

Franklin had learned that oil can make water calm. He showed them that his cane was hollow. He had filled it with oil. He had made the water still by sprinkling oil on it.

Franklin was in England for nine years. He worked hard to keep peace between England and the colonies. Americans were becoming more and more angry over English laws and taxes. The English were angry too. They said the colonies were English. So they should obey English laws.

On January 30, 1774, some of the most important men in the English government held a meeting.

Franklin was there. He tried to tell them how the Americans felt. But the English were too angry to listen. They did not want to believe anything Franklin had to say. So they blamed him for all the troubles in the colonies. They called him a liar. They said he was the "Master of Mischief."

Franklin stood before them, pale and silent. He wanted to tell them there might be a war between the colonies and

England. But he knew they would not listen. Franklin left the meeting, sad and alone.

Then bad news came from home. Deborah had died. Franklin decided to go back. He had done all that he could in England. In the spring of 1775 he set sail for America.

12

THE AMERICAN REVOLUTION

On April 19, 1775, American and English soldiers fired on each other near Boston. War had begun. It was the American Revolution.

Franklin reached Philadelphia on May 5. He was 69 years old. William was married. Sally was married and had children. Franklin was now a grand-father.

Franklin was soon back at work. He went to the Continental Congress.

The Continental Congress was a meeting of leaders from all over the colonies. They met to decide what should be done about the war.

Franklin was the oldest man at the congress. He was also one of the busiest. He was postmaster general of America. He was put in charge of printing money. He wrote to friends in England and France asking for help. And he worked on one of the most important papers in history.

The paper was the Declaration of Independence. It said England no longer ruled the colonies. It said they were now the 13 "united States of America." On July 4, 1776, Congress agreed to sign it.

The war went on. The English were winning most of the battles. Their soldiers were well fed. They had guns and uniforms. The Americans were dressed in rags. They did not have enough guns or food.

America had to have help. The men in Congress thought they might get it from France. France did not like England. And if America won the war, France would have a strong new friend.

The men in Congress decided to ask Franklin to go to France. They hoped he might get the French to give some help.

It was hard to leave home again. But Franklin knew he had to go.

In December of 1776 Franklin left for France. He tried to go secretly. He knew English spies were watching him. He knew the English would try to capture him. And he knew that if they did, they would hang him.

It was a cold and stormy trip. And Franklin was an old man. When he got to France he was tired and sick. There was no one to meet him. His trip was so secret, no one knew he was coming.

13

THE FRENCH LOVE FRANKLIN

Franklin hired a coach to take him to the city of Paris. The roads were very bad. Franklin often had to stop the coach and rest.

The news that Franklin was coming traveled fast. As he neared Paris he was surprised to see hundreds of people lining the way. Their cheers and smiles made him feel much better. In Paris he was met by a great crowd. They were all waving and cheering.

Franklin was asked everywhere. He went to parties and great balls. He talked to the people in the streets. He talked to the king in the palace. Everywhere he went, he made new friends for America.

The French loved Franklin. There were hundreds of pictures painted of him. The big fur hat he liked to wear became famous. French women curled up their hair to look like Franklin's hat.

Franklin was working hard to get help

from the French government. But the Americans were still losing battles. The French thought they might lose the war.

Then Franklin heard good news. The Americans had won a big battle. Franklin hoped the French would send help now. And they did!

The French sent money for guns and food. They sent men. And they sent ships. One ship was given to a young American captain named John Paul Jones. He named it the *Bonhomme Richard,* after Franklin's almanac. In it he won America's first sea battle with the English.

The war lasted for six long years. Then, in October of 1781, there was a great battle. The Americans and the French beat the English. It was the last important battle of the war.

The Revolution was over at last. The Americans had won.

14

HOME AT LAST

In the summer of 1785 Franklin came home to Philadelphia. He had come to the city as a poor young boy 62 years before. He was now 79 years old. And he was famous all over the world.

Philadelphia went wild with joy. Crowds cheered. Church bells rang. Cannons roared. The great man was home at last.

Franklin went to live with Sally and

her children. And he went on working for his country.

America was a new country. It needed a new government. In 1787 men from the different states met in Philadelphia. They met to plan the government. This plan was the Constitution of the United States.

Benjamin Franklin was one of the men sent by Pennsylvania.

There were arguments. Each man had different ideas. But Franklin was good at making people work together. The men listened to him. At last the Constitution was signed by everyone.

This was the last great act of his life. Franklin was old and tired. He stayed home most of the time. He read books. He wrote letters to his friends in France and England. He played with his grandchildren. He taught the little ones how to read.

On the night of April 17, 1790, Benjamin Franklin died quietly in his sleep. He was 84 years old.

The death of this great and good man was mourned by people all over the world. He had been the most brilliant and best-loved American of his time.